SUSAN AND JAMES PATTERSON

Illustrated by
HSINPING PAN

BIG WORDS for little geniuses

Arachibutyrophobia

(Ah-RACK-ee-byoo-tee-ro-FO-bee-ya)

Arachibutyrophobia is the **alarming** fear of peanut butter sticking to the top of your mouth!

Bibliomania (bib-lee-oh-MAY-nee-ah)

You have **bibliomania** if you love to collect as many **books** as you can.

Catawampus (ca-tah-WOMP-us)

Catawampus means tilted, diagonal, or just a little bit **crooked**.

Dulcifluous (dull-SIH-floo-iss)

The **delightful** word **dulcifluous** sounds like what it means: flowing sweetly and gently.

Empyreal (em-pie-REE-ul)

Empyreal means heavenly, like the **enchanting** blue color of the sky on a sunny day.

Flibbertigibbet (flih-ber-tee-JIH-bit)

A **friend** who loves to talk and talk can be called a **flibbertigibbet**.

Gobbledygook (GAH-bul-dee-gook)

If you hear words that sound a little **goofy** or nonsensical, you're listening to **gobbledygook**!

WHACKA

Doodle dooooooo

SHOOKA wooka looka

HARGA PARGA mumsy lay

Lumsy oogly Gobbeldy ooo

Earf..omie googly

BAR TARSH

Boomie loomie

YARZOOMIE MAIA CHANCA

Horripilation (haw-rih-puh-LAY-shun)

If you're cold, scared, or excited, you may get **horripilation**, or goose bumps, on your **head** or body.

Idioglossia *(ih-dee-oh-GLOH-see-ya)*

If you share a secret language with a friend, it's called an **idioglossia**.

Juxtaposition (jucks-ta-poe-ZIH-shun)

When you put things side by side, you've **just** made a **juxtaposition**!

Kerfuffle (kerr-FUH-ful)

Have you ever **kicked** up a big fuss about something, like baking a cake? That's called a **kerfuffle**!

Lilliputian (li-lee-PYOO-shun)

Lilliputian means very tiny or **little**, especially when describing a person.

Magnanimous (mag-NA-nih-mus)

If you're **magnanimous**, you like to share your **most** favorite toys with your friends.

Nincompoop (NIN-come-poop)

When you're acting a little silly or **naughty**, you may be called a **nincompoop**!

Onomatopoeia (AH-noh-ma-toe-PEE-ya)

An **onomatopoeia** is a sound word, like moo, splat, and **oink**!
Can you think of any others?

Pulchritudinous (puhl-kri-TOO-dih-nus)

Pretty and **pulchritudinous** mean the same thing, but one is much more fun to say!

Quokka (KWOH-ka)

The **quokka** is called the happiest animal in the world because it smiles **quite** a lot!

Rapscallion (rap-SKALL-yen)

A **rapscallion** is someone who **really** likes to cause trouble.

Stelliferous (stell-IH-fur-us)

When the night sky is filled with **stars**, it's a **stelliferous sight**!

Tokus (TOOK-us)

Your **tokus** has lots of funny-sounding names, like heinie, **tush**, and bum-bum!

Undulating (UN-dyoo-lay-ting)

Something that moves **up** and down is **undulating**, like the waves of the ocean.

Volitant (VOLL-ih-tint)

It would feel **very** exciting to be **volitant** and fly through the air like a bird.

Whirligig (WHIR-lee-gig)

A **whirligig** spins around and around, like a pinwheel in the **wind**.

Xanthochroism (*zan-THOCK-ro-ih-zim*)

Animals that have **xanthochroism** are bright yellow or orange, like goldfish.

Yaffingale *(YAH-fin-gale)*

A **yaffingale** is a colorful bird with **yellow** and green feathers on its body and red on top of its head.

Zamboni (zam-BO-nee)

Zamboni is the name of the big machine that **zooms** around an ice rink to smooth out the ice.

Here are more BIG WORDS for you to learn.

Adamantine *(a-dah-MAN-teen)* — unbreakable

Bumfuzzle *(BUM-fuzz-ul)* — to confuse someone

Collywobbles *(CALL-ee-woh-bulls)* — a tummyache

Discombobulate *(dis-come-BOB-yoo-late)* — to confuse someone

Erinaceous *(air-in-AY-shuss)* — having to do with or looking like a hedgehog

Felicitations *(feh-liss-ih-TAY-shuns)* — kind words to make people feel happy

Grandiloquence *(gran-DIH-loh-kwens)* — using big words or lots of style

Humongous *(hyoo-MUN-gus)* — very, very large

Isthmus *(ISS-muss)* — a thin strip of land that connects two bigger areas of land

Jillion *(JILL-yun)* — a very high number

Kumquat *(COME-kwat)* — a sweet orange-colored fruit

Loquacious *(low-KWAY-shuss)* — very talkative

Moppet *(MOH-pet)* — a young child

Nephelococcygia *(NEH-fell-oh-kok-SIH-jee-uh)* — finding familiar shapes in clouds

Which is the most fun word to say?

Ozostomia *(oh-zo-STO-mee-ya)* — bad-smelling breath

Pandiculation *(pan-dik-yoo-LAY-shun)* — stretching and yawning at the same time

Quixotic *(kwik-SAW-tick)* — when you think that your dreams can come true

Rigmarole *(RIG-ma-roll)* — something that is complicated and takes a long time

Syzygy *(SIH-zih-jee)* — when objects are lined up, especially the sun, the moon, and the earth

Tarradiddle *(tare-ah-DIH-dul)* — a small fib

Uxorious *(ucks-OH-ree-us)* — very much in love with one's wife

Vichyssoise *(vih-shee-SWAHZ)* — a creamy soup made with potatoes and onions

Whangdoodle *(WANG-doo-dull)* — an imaginary creature from children's books

Xylophone *(ZY-lo-fone)* — a musical instrument played by hitting wooden bars

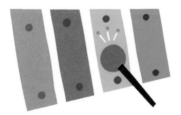

Yarnwindle *(YARN-win-dill)* — a tool for winding yarn into a ball

Zoosemiotics *(zoe-ah-seh-mee-AW-ticks)* — the study of how animals communicate, like birds singing and dogs wagging their tails